MOVIE FAVORITES

Solos and Band Arrangements
Correlated with Essential Elements Band Method

Arranged by
MICHAEL SWEENEY

Welcome to Essential Elements Movie Favorites! There are two versions of each selection in this versatile book. The SOLO version appears on the left-hand page of your book. The FULL BAND arrangement appears on the right-hand page. Optional accompaniment recordings are available separately in CD or cassette format. Use these recordings when playing solos for friends and family.

ISBN 978-0-7935-5961-9

HAL•LEONARD™ CORPORATION

7777 W. BLUEMOUND RD. P.O. BOX 13819 MILWAUKEE, WI 53213

Theme From "JURASSIC PARK"

B♭ BASS CLARINET
Solo

Composed by JOHN WILLIAMS
Arranged by MICHAEL SWEENEY

MCA music publishing

Theme From "JURASSIC PARK"

B♭ BASS CLARINET
Band Arrangement

Composed by JOHN WILLIAMS
Arranged by MICHAEL SWEENEY

MCA music publishing

From CHARIOTS OF FIRE
CHARIOTS OF FIRE

B♭ BASS CLARINET
Solo

Music by VANGELIS
Arranged by MICHAEL SWEENEY

CHARIOTS OF FIRE

Bb BASS CLARINET
Band Arrangement

Music by VANGELIS
Arranged by MICHAEL SWEENEY

00860017

From THE MAN FROM SNOWY RIVER

THE MAN FROM SNOWY RIVER

(Main Title Theme)

By BRUCE ROWLAND
Arranged by MICHAEL SWEENEY

B♭ BASS CLARINET
Solo

00860017

From THE MAN FROM SNOWY RIVER

THE MAN FROM SNOWY RIVER
(Main Title Theme)

By BRUCE ROWLAND
Arranged by MICHAEL SWEENEY

Bb **BASS CLARINET**
Band Arrangement

00860017

From The Paramount Motion Picture FORREST GUMP

FORREST GUMP - MAIN TITLE
(Feather Theme)

Bb BASS CLARINET
Solo

Music by ALAN SILVESTRI
Arranged by MICHAEL SWEENEY

00860017

FORREST GUMP - MAIN TITLE
(Feather Theme)

Bᵇ BASS CLARINET
Band Arrangement

Music by ALAN SILVESTRI
Arranged by MICHAEL SWEENEY

00860017

From AN AMERICAN TAIL
SOMEWHERE OUT THERE

Words and Music by JAMES HORNER,
BARRY MANN and CYNTHIA WEIL
Arranged by MICHAEL SWEENEY

B♭ BASS CLARINET
Solo

MCA music publishing

From AN AMERICAN TAIL

SOMEWHERE OUT THERE

B♭ BASS CLARINET
Band Arrangement

Words and Music by JAMES HORNER,
BARRY MANN and CYNTHIA WEIL
Arranged by MICHAEL SWEENEY

From DANCES WITH WOLVES
THE JOHN DUNBAR THEME

Bᵇ BASS CLARINET
Solo

By JOHN BARRY
Arranged by MICHAEL SWEENEY

THE JOHN DUNBAR THEME

B♭ BASS CLARINET
Band Arrangement

By JOHN BARRY
Arranged by MICHAEL SWEENEY

00860017

From The Paramount Motion Picture RAIDERS OF THE LOST ARK

RAIDERS MARCH

B♭ **BASS CLARINET**
Solo

By JOHN WILLIAMS
Arranged by MICHAEL SWEENEY

RAIDERS MARCH

B♭ **BASS CLARINET**
Band Arrangement

By JOHN WILLIAMS
Arranged by MICHAEL SWEENEY

00860017

From APOLLO 13
APOLLO 13
(End Credits)

By JAMES HORNER
Arranged by MICHAEL SWEENEY

B♭ BASS CLARINET
Solo

MCA music publishing

APOLLO 13

(End Credits)

Bb BASS CLARINET
Band Arrangement

By JAMES HORNER
Arranged by MICHAEL SWEENEY

MCA music publishing

00860017

THEME FROM E.T. (THE EXTRA-TERRESTRIAL)

B♭ BASS CLARINET
Solo

Music by JOHN WILLIAMS
Arranged by MICHAEL SWEENEY

MCA music publishing

THEME FROM E.T. (THE EXTRA-TERRESTRIAL)

B♭ **BASS CLARINET**
Band Arrangement

Music by JOHN WILLIAMS
Arranged by MICHAEL SWEENEY

MCA music publishing

Theme From The Paramount Picture STAR TREK

STAR TREK® - THE MOTION PICTURE

B♭ **BASS CLARINET**
Solo

Music by JERRY GOLDSMITH
Arranged by MICHAEL SWEENEY

00860017

STAR TREK®-THE- MOTION PICTURE

Bb BASS CLARINET
Band Arrangement

Music by JERRY GOLDSMITH
Arranged by MICHAEL SWEENEY

00860017

From The Universal Motion Picture BACK TO THE FUTURE

BACK TO THE FUTURE

B♭ BASS CLARINET
Solo

By ALAN SILVESTRI
Arranged by MICHAEL SWEENEY

MCA music publishing

BACK TO THE FUTURE

Bb **BASS CLARINET**
Band Arrangement

By ALAN SILVESTRI
Arranged by MICHAEL SWEENEY